IWO JIMA
AND OKINAWA

by

Wallace B. Black
and
Jean F. Blashfield

CRESTWOOD HOUSE
New York

Maxwell Macmillan Canada
Toronto

Maxwell Macmillan International
New York Oxford Singapore Sydney

Library of Congress Cataloging-in-Publication Data

Black, Wallace B.
   Iwo Jima and Okinawa / by Wallace B. Black and Jean F. Blashfield. —
1st ed.
     p.   cm. — (World War II 50th anniversary series)
Includes index.
   Summary: Recounts the brutal battles between the U.S. troops and the
Japanese on the islands of Iwo Jima and Okinawa during World War II.
   ISBN 0-89686-569-X
   1. Iwo Jima, Battle of, 1945 — Juvenile literature. 2. Okinawa Island
(Japan) — History — Juvenile literature. 3. World War, 1939-1945 —
Campaigns — Japan — Okinawa Island — Juvenile literature. [1. Iwo Jima,
Battle of, 1945. 2. Okinawa Island (Japan) — History. 3. World War,
1939-1945 — Campaigns — Japan — Okinawa Island.] I. Blashfield, Jean F.
II. Title. III. Series: Black, Wallace B.
World War II 50th anniversary.
D767.99.I9B57   1993
940.54'26—dc20

                92-25868

Created and produced by B & B Publishing, Inc.

Picture Credits
Dave Conant (map) - page 20
National Archives - pages 3, 4, 9, 11, 13, 14, 17, 18, 19, 23, 25, 27, 29, 31, 35, 37, 41, 42, 43, 44 (all),
   45 (all)
United States Navy - pages 7, 12, 15, 33, 38

CRESTWOOD
HOUSE

Macmillan Publishing Company
866 Third Avenue
New York, NY 10022

Maxwell Macmillan Canada, Inc.
1200 Eglinton Avenue East
Suite 200
Don Mills, Ontario M3C 3N1

Macmillan Publishing Company is part of the Maxwell Communication Group of Companies.

Printed in the United States of America

First Edition

10 9 8 7 6 5 4 3 2 1

CONTENTS

The big guns on battleships and cruisers are joined by 40mm guns in bombarding enemy targets prior to the landings by U.S. Marines on Iwo Jima.

Chapter 1

ISLAND HOPPING

Six hundred and fifty miles south of Japan lies a small group of islands known as the Bonin Islands or the Volcano Islands. The largest of these is a pork chop-shaped island called Iwo Jima. Claimed by the Japanese in 1861, it was sparsely settled by a few Americans, Portuguese, Englishmen, Hawaiians and Japanese. All became Japanese citizens.

During World War I Japanese army and navy bases were established there. In 1944, finally realizing that U.S. forces were moving rapidly northward as they "island hopped" across the Pacific, the Japanese made Iwo Jima a key base and reinforced it further.

By 1945 Japanese Zero fighters based there were not only attacking and destroying large numbers of American B-29s that were bombing Japan as they passed near Iwo Jima, but they were attacking the B-29 airfields in the Mariana Islands as well.

From the U.S. point of view, the tiny island of Iwo Jima had to be captured and its airfields and defending forces destroyed. Soon to become a bloody battlefield, Iwo Jima was the last island target in the U.S. island-hopping campaign.

The Pacific War Begins

December 7, 1941, the day of the Japanese sneak attack on Pearl Harbor in Hawaii, marked the beginning of World War II for the United States and of almost four years of war with Japan. The U.S. Army and Navy experienced one humiliating defeat after another from Pearl Harbor to the surrender of the Philippine Islands on May 6, 1942.

The allies of the United States—Great Britain, France and the Netherlands—also suffered severe losses. In less than six months' time the Japanese invading forces captured Burma, the Malay peninsula, Singapore, Thailand, French Indochina and Hong Kong on the mainland of southeast Asia. They also occupied islands of the Dutch East Indies and numerous other Pacific islands.

Australia Threatened

With the surrender of the Dutch East Indies and the Philippines, the Japanese military forces rolled on. Their next targets were Papua New Guinea and the huge island continent of Australia itself.

Under the command of General Douglas MacArthur, 25,000 newly arrived American troops and 250,000 Australian civilian soldiers made ready to defend Australia against an invasion.

Following the defeat at Pearl Harbor, the U.S. Navy was greatly outnumbered by the Japanese Imperial Navy. However, to stop the further Japanese advances toward Australia, the U.S. aircraft carriers *Lexington* and *Yorktown* sailed from Pearl Harbor on April 30, 1942, to take up positions in the Coral Sea northeast of Australia.

Battles of Coral Sea and Midway

Receiving word that an invasion fleet was approaching Port Moresby in New Guinea, the U.S. carriers set out to locate and attack the enemy. Under the command of Admiral Frank J. Fletcher, the U.S. flattops engaged the Japanese in the Coral Sea. Following a fierce two-day aerial battle on May 7 and 8, the large Japanese naval force and the Port Moresby invasion fleet were turned back. The U.S. carrier *Lexington* was sunk. The Japanese lost one light carrier and another carrier was badly damaged.

Just one month later Japanese Admiral Isoroku Yama-

The USS Yorktown *sinking following the battle of Midway. While the loss of one flattop was a blow to the U.S. forces, the Japanese lost four carriers during the battle.*

moto, commander in chief of the Japanese Combined Fleets, led an invasion force accompanied by four carriers to invade Midway Island. The Japanese also planned to attack the Hawaiian Islands, Alaska and the west coast of the United States.

Again U.S. aircraft carriers came to the rescue. On June 4, three U.S. flattops intercepted and attacked the four Japanese aircraft carriers. All four Japanese flattops were sunk with the loss of one U.S. carrier, the *Yorktown*. Midway Island was not invaded. Admiral Yamamoto, realizing that the battle was lost, cancelled the mission.

The Battle of Midway marked a major turning point in the war in the Pacific. Although the United States lost some 300 pilots and air crew members and 150 planes, the U.S. Navy had proven its superiority over the Japanese. The time had come to strike back at the Japanese.

Island Hopping Begins

The United States planned to advance from one island group to the next on the way northward toward Japan. Guadalcanal in the Solomon Islands was the first island target. The U.S. Marines landed there on August 7, 1942, and drove the Japanese from the island in February 1943. It was a long and bloody campaign with heavy casualties on both sides.

The next stops in the island-hopping plan called for attacking the Japanese in New Guinea and capturing the island of New Georgia in the Solomon chain. These actions were part of a plan to capture Rabaul, the Japanese headquarters in the South Pacific on the island of New Britain. However, Rabaul was bypassed and islands farther north were attacked.

Gilberts, Marshalls and Marianas Captured

Admiral Chester W. Nimitz, commander of the Central Pacific Fleet, sent the U.S. 5th Fleet commanded by Admiral Raymond Spruance against the Gilbert Islands and the Marshall Islands. They fell to marine landing forces in November 1943 and February 1944. The Japanese forces on these and other islands were wiped out to the last man. The cost in American lives was also heavy but the island-hopping plan was succeeding.

The U.S. 5th Fleet then moved on to invade and capture the Mariana Islands in the central Pacific. In the Battle of the Philippine Sea the Japanese suffered another great defeat as they lost three more aircraft carriers and hundreds of planes and pilots. The U.S. Marines, fighting costly battles, captured the islands of Tinian, Saipan and Guam in the Marianas.

More Japanese Islands Fall

In the southwestern Pacific General MacArthur's forces captured all of New Guinea. Fighting northward against

U.S. Marines firing across a smoking no-man's land on a Pacific island. As the U.S. forces island hopped across the Pacific they conquered one island after another from Guadalcanal to Okinawa.

strong Japanese resistance, MacArthur's forces landed on the island of Leyte in the Philippines in October of 1944 and Luzon in January 1945.

Iwo Jima Next in Line

With the capture of these islands the United States now controlled airfields that put the U.S. Army Air Force (USAAF) within bombing range of the main islands of Japan. But one small island stood in the way. It was the last stop in the long island-hopping campaign that extended for 3,000 miles north from the Solomon Islands. It was the tiny island of Iwo Jima, over 600 miles from Japan.

Chapter 2

TARGET
IWO JIMA

On October 3, 1944, the decision was made that Iwo Jima must be captured and used as an American air base. At the same time, General MacArthur was ordered to complete the capture of the Philippines. United States forces were then to prepare for a landing on the huge Japanese island of Okinawa.

The U.S. Navy and Marine Corps were assigned the task of attacking and capturing Iwo Jima. Admiral Nimitz would plan and carry out what would become one of the bloodiest battles of the Pacific war.

U.S. Navy, Marine and Army specialists planned the assault. A huge fleet of 73 troop transports was to carry the assault force and its supplies from Hawaii to a landing on Iwo Jima. Some 80,000 U.S. Marines were to carry out the actual invasion. Warships and aircraft of all types would provide support from the sea and in the air.

The U.S. Plan of Attack

Task Force 53 under the command of Rear Admiral Harry W. Hill would see that the marines got to Iwo Jima. This giant force carried over 1,000 pounds of supplies for each of the 80,000 marines in the invasion force. Everything from millions of rounds of ammunition to enough food to feed a large city for a month was on board.

Task Force 52 under the command of Admiral W. H. P. Blandy was made up of battleships, cruisers, aircraft carriers and support vessels. They had the job of softening up

Pre-invasion briefings of U.S. Marine unit commanders were held on every ship that carried the marines to the shores of Iwo Jima.

the beachhead on Iwo Jima. The island was a giant fortress. Its heavy guns were hidden in blockhouses, pillboxes and caves on Mount Suribachi at the south end of the island and throughout the rest of that eight-square-mile piece of land.

The navy was to blast the enemy's defenses and air-fields with broadsides of high explosives from the big guns of the attacking fleet and tons of bombs from bombers and fighters. They were to be helped by bombers of the USAAF flying from the Marianas.

The marine attack force was under the command of Lieutenant General Holland M. "Howlin' Mad" Smith. A veteran of two wars, at age 62 he was one of the oldest combat generals in the armed services. He was beloved and respected by his marines.

After months of preparation and many delays, everything was ready and a final date was set. On February 19, 1945, the U.S. Marines would begin landing on the beaches of Iwo Jima.

Iwo Jima Bombardment Begins

During early December U.S. Navy warships began shelling Iwo Jima. For some 72 days the tiny island was hit again and again by tons of bombs dropped by navy and army air force planes and by heavy shelling from the warships of Task Force 52.

General Smith and his staff wanted at least 10 days of concentrated bombardment preceding the landings on February 19. But they were only allotted four. There were not enough ships and ammunition to support the landings in Iwo Jima and the campaign in the Philippines at the same time. "Howlin' Mad" Smith howled repeatedly for more and heavier bombardment. Without it he predicted slaughter of his marines on the beaches of Iwo Jima.

TBM and SB2C bombers from the aircraft carrier USS Essex *unload their bombs on Iwo Jima prior to the invasion.*

Iva Toguri, an American-born Japanese known as Tokyo Rose, being interviewed after the war. She made continuous broadcasts to American troops in an effort to lower the morale of the invasion troops.

The Japanese Defenders

The Japanese began to fortify Iwo Jima in 1944. They knew that it was a vital base for the defense of Japan. Lieutenant General Tadamichi Kuribayashi was in charge. He commanded a force of some 22,000 Japanese army and navy troops. He reinforced the high ground at both ends of the island so that he could fire on all approaches. Most of the defenses were underground so that they could resist even the heaviest bombardment.

Japanese spies had already learned that Iwo Jima was to be invaded. "Tokyo Rose," an English-speaking radio announcer, broadcast the names of specific marine units. Americans were horrified at how much the Japanese knew. It is no wonder the Japanese were well prepared and inflicted terrible casualties on the marines as they landed.

D-Day Minus Three

In the early morning hours of February 16, Admiral Blandy's force began three days of bombardment, not the four days promised. At 8:00 A.M. the order to commence firing was given. Six giant battleships, five heavy cruisers and numerous destroyers opened fire. Ten aircraft carriers launched aerial attacks against the Japanese island.

Specific targets had been assigned. However, weather was bad that first day and targets were missed and aircraft missions were cancelled. B-24s from Saipan had to return to their bases without dropping a bomb. Of almost 1,000 targets only a few dozen had actually been destroyed. The first day's "softening up" was a failure.

On D-Day minus two the weather was clear and the U.S. forces unleashed their full power. Some 12,000 rounds of shells and rockets poured onto the island's defenses. Carrier aircraft dropped tons of bombs and strafed the beaches with machine guns and rockets. Planes dropped tanks filled with napalm (a mixture of gasoline and chemicals) on key targets. But General Kuribayashi's forces fired back at the attacking forces with deadly accuracy. When the results of the day's bombings were analyzed, it was found that most of the Japanese defenses had hardly been touched.

U.S. Marines in landing craft circle off Iwo Jima as a giant U.S. battleship blasts Japanese targets on shore.

A U.S. Navy cruiser adds a barrage of rockets to the 12,000 tons of explosives unloaded on Iwo Jima before D-Day.

Admiral Blandy asked for a 24-hour delay in the landing but it was refused. The weather again turned bad, but Admiral Blandy did not hold back. He ordered every ship to commence firing. For the entire third day they raked the island with all the firepower they could command. Battleships, cruisers and rocket-firing craft poured tons of explosives onto the eastern shore of Iwo Jima where the landings were to take place.

Admiral Blandy's forces had done all they could to prepare the way. As darkness fell, all grew silent as the marines on the transports and landing craft made final preparations. Many read a little prayer that had been passed out by navy and marine chaplains. Composed in England in the 1640s, it read:

"Lord! I shall be verie busy this day.

I may forget Thee, but do not Thou forget me."

Chapter 3

D-DAY ON IWO JIMA

The original group of 73 transports that had left Hawaii months earlier had now grown to some 500 ships. Battleships, aircraft carriers, troop transports and landing craft of every type circled around Iwo Jima. In the pre-dawn hours on February 19 the marines were wakened as loudspeakers blared out the wakeup call — reveille! At 6:30, as the sun rose in the east, Vice-Admiral Richmond K. Turner, commander of all Iwo Jima invasion forces, gave the order to launch the landing force.

H-Hour, the time the marines were to hit the beach, was scheduled for 9:00 A.M. The final pre-landing bombardment of the beaches began. For over two hours every naval warship available—some 75 battleships, cruisers and destroyers—unleashed a blistering barrage onto the landing area. Rocket-firing ships launched some 10,000 of their fiery missiles toward the cliffs and high ground surrounding the east beaches.

After two hours of naval bombardment, navy aircraft took over. In screaming dives squadrons of Corsair and Hellcat fighters bombed and strafed target areas. Dive-bombers unloaded their heavy bombs. After dropping their deadly cargo, the attacking aircraft withdrew and the naval bombardment continued. Landing craft circling a few miles out finally headed for shore.

Marines Hit the Beach

The final barrage from the warships offshore lifted and moved inland to hit other targets at 8:57 A.M. The first ma-

Landing craft bring the first wave of marines to the black sands of Iwo Jima.

rines landed at 9:02 on the two-mile-long beaches at the southeast shore of the island in the shadow of 556-foot-tall Mount Suribachi.

The first units to land were some 70 amphibious tractors called amtracs. They each carried a 75mm howitzer and several machine guns and a crew of three. Their job was to land and commence firing on any enemy defenses near the landing zones. They reached the two-mile-long beachhead easily. Grinding forward through the black sand of Iwo Jima they commenced firing.

Japanese fire was very light. Their antiaircraft guns were concentrating on the fighters and bombers that were strafing just ahead of the landing force. General Kuribayashi had issued orders to hold off firing on the marines until there was a heavy concentration of enemy on the beaches. A few minutes behind the amtracs the first wave of troop-carrying landing craft came ashore. Their ramps dropped and the first 1,400 marine infantry surged onto the shores of Iwo Jima.

Following at five-minute intervals wave after wave of additional landing craft hit the beach. Resistance by the Japanese was light although there were some U.S. casualties. The heavy sand beaches made movement difficult and it was almost impossible to dig fox holes. Each man carried equipment and ammunition weighing as much as 100 pounds, making any movement difficult.

Soon over 6,000 marines were on the beach. General Kuribayashi watched carefully, still holding his fire. His plan of attack was taking shape while he waited for the beaches to fill up. As the marines started to move inland, fire from the ships and attacking planes stopped or moved to targets farther inland. It was time for the Japanese general to spring his trap.

Japanese Unleash Deadly Attack

At 10:00 A.M. the Japanese unleashed their attack as planned. Hidden machine gun pits came to life and sprayed the beach with a heavy crossfire. Hundreds of mortars

Marines of the 5th Division inch their way up a slope on Red Beach toward Mount Suribachi as the smoke of battle drifts over them.

Marines burrow into the volcanic black sand on the beach of Iwo Jima. The coarse sand clogged weapons caused temporary blindness and got into wounds.

began to fire from hidden reinforced concrete pits. Big guns hidden on Mount Suribachi unloaded their giant shells all along the beaches and on the landing craft offshore. Every part of the two-mile-long strip of sand was under heavy fire. The marines had no place to hide and many were slaughtered on the spot.

Landing craft still continued to speed toward shore. Dozens were hit and sunk. Others landed more men, tanks, light artillery, bulldozers and supplies. Casualties were

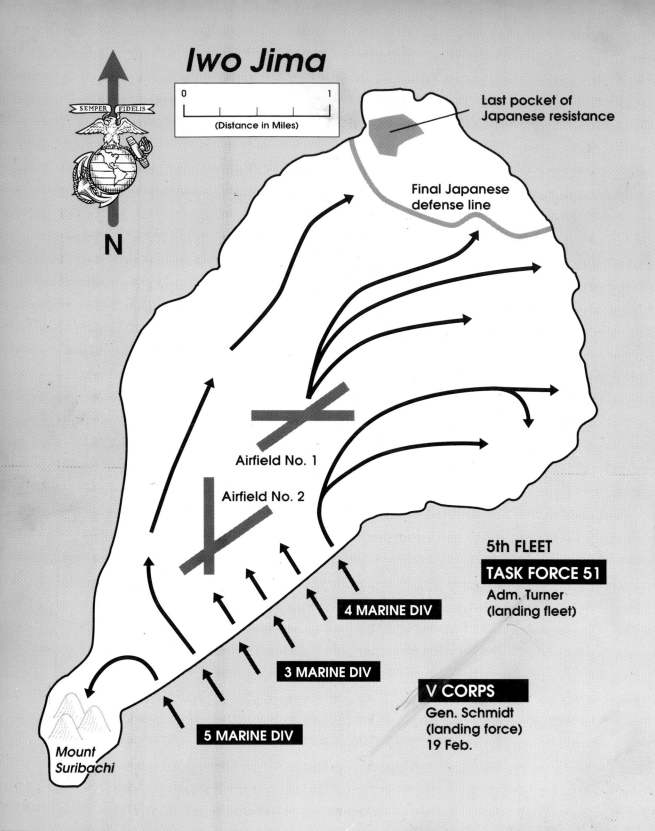

Iwo Jima

Last pocket of Japanese resistance

Final Japanese defense line

0   1

(Distance in Miles)

N

SEMPER FIDELIS

Airfield No. 1

Airfield No. 2

5th FLEET

TASK FORCE 51

Adm. Turner
(landing fleet)

4 MARINE DIV

3 MARINE DIV

V CORPS

Gen. Schmidt
(landing force)
19 Feb.

5 MARINE DIV

Mount Suribachi

heavy. But the tough marines kept slowly driving forward and fighting fiercely. There was no room to maneuver and retreat was impossible. All the brave marines could do was fight or die.

The Japanese general, though, had waited too long to start his attack. If he had blasted the marines as they were landing, he would have stopped the invasion in its tracks. As it was, the marines had landed over 6,000 men along with some Sherman tanks and enough artillery to begin to fight back. In spite of the death-dealing attacks by the Japanese the marines advanced slowly inland.

Traffic Jam on the Beaches

By midday the beach was a mass of struggling humanity and equipment. It was impossible for landing craft to reach the shore amidst craft that had been sunk and wrecked equipment. The entire beachhead was filled with marines— alive and dead—as well as supplies and wreckage. At 1:00 P.M. further landings were called off until the situation ashore improved.

In spite of this, by the end of day one, several units had fought their way across the southern tip of the island. They had advanced only about 350 yards but they were now able to attack Mount Suribachi to the south and the island's main airfield to the north. More landing craft finally were able to land. Reinforcements kept coming and the marines continued to advance slowly inland to the west and north.

By nightfall the marines had established a solid line of defense and had advanced inland to the main airfield. Their losses had been terrible. One unit that landed with nearly 1,000 men had only about 300 still alive, uninjured and able to fight. Twenty-four marine infantry battalions had landed on that fateful February 19. The average casualty figure for each of those battalions would be 687 dead and wounded. By day's end 566 marines had been killed and approximately 1,800 had been wounded.

Chapter 4

MOUNT SURIBACHI CAPTURED

Mount Suribachi had been cut off from the rest of the island on the first day. However, it was still occupied by a strong force of heavily armed Japanese. They could still fire at targets across the length of the island or fire directly down onto the marines on the beaches below.

As day one drew to a close, some 30,000 marines and mountains of supplies had been landed. Brigadier General Leo D. Hermle was the ranking officer on the island. Arriving late in the day he realized how badly things were going. The beach was still jammed. Casualties were extremely high and objectives had not been reached. He closed down operations for the night. Expecting suicidal banzai charges from the Japanese during the night, the marines were surprised. General Kuribayashi felt that suicidal charges were not called for against a huge invasion force. Instead the Japanese merely continued to fire their mortars and artillery throughout the night.

Marines Try to Bring Order Out of Chaos

On the beaches, using bulldozers and tanks, marines began to clear the huge traffic jam. They moved supplies inland, shoved wrecks into the sea, and cleared paths from the beaches. They carved supply dumps out of the sand and rock and cut roadways so that tanks and trucks could move inland. Many of the dead and wounded had been evacuated

Smashed by Japanese mortar and shell fire, amtracs and other vehicles lay knocked out on the black sands of Iwo Jima. Mount Suribachi looms in the background.

during day one but hundreds more were still trapped on the beaches that night.

In preparation for the next day's battles the warships offshore kept up a constant bombardment. Their goal was to soften up and damage the main Japanese defenses in the center and on the northern portion of the island.

As the marines huddled in foxholes waiting for dawn, the Japanese attacked. Hand-to-hand fighting occurred again and again throughout the long night. Hand grenades, bayonets and small arms were brought into play. The Japanese were trying to regain lost ground. It was a bloody night filled with gunfire, explosions and cries of the wounded.

Day Two Sees Battles on Two Fronts

The first effort on the morning of February 20 was to evacuate the dead and wounded. The second major effort was to make room for new arrivals and to prepare for the day's offensive. Wrecked jeeps, artillery, bulldozers and tanks were scattered everywhere. Battle-torn and blood-stained equipment of the dead and wounded cluttered the beaches. But as the morning wore on planned attacks began to get underway.

On the south end of the island three battalions of the 28th Marines were given the task of conquering Mount Suribachi. Under the command of Harry B. "Harry the Horse" Liversedge, they formed a line across the narrow island and began their slow fight toward the smoking mountain. Fired upon from strong points on Suribachi, they were under fire from their rear as well.

General Kuribayashi had known that Mount Suribachi would be an immediate target of the U.S. attackers. This highest point on the island was a perfect observation post. From the peak of Suribachi fire control officers directed Japanese guns stationed on all points on the island against the invading marines.

Mount Suribachi Heavily Defended

Manned by 2,000 Japanese troops, Mount Suribachi was a huge fortress. Caves and tunnels ran through the giant rock from top to bottom. There were hundreds of concrete blockhouses, mortar pits and machine gun nests. Its defenders were ready to fight to the death.

Attacks by the marines to the west and to the north of the mountain began at 8:30 A.M. on the morning of day two. Heavy bombardment and air attacks unloaded tons of high explosives on Mount Suribachi and the enemy positions just to the north. The Japanese fought back with heavy mortar and artillery barrages. With accurate defensive fire directed by spotters on the peak of Suribachi the marines were suffering heavy casualties.

The marines' plan to capture Mount Suribachi was a simple one as described by one marine officer. "A frontal attack, surround the base, locate a route up, then climb it!" The problem was that the Japanese defenders could spot

The smoke of battle rolls over Mount Suribachi as the marines prepare for their final assault.

every move the marines made. Scattered pockets of Japanese soldiers hidden at ground level directly in the path of the advancing marines also ambushed the marines. Marine units supporting Colonel Liversedge's attackers used grenades, flamethrowers and satchel charges of high explosive to blast out the hidden Japanese defenders still fighting in their midst.

Marine tanks and 155mm howitzers were finally brought into action by the end of the day. They suffered heavy losses but were still able to fight. Once they entered the battle though, they helped the 28th Marines open the way to the base of Mount Suribachi.

Most Decorated Platoon in Marine History

On day three the 28th Marines continued to fight their way toward the base of Mount Suribachi. By day's end over 1,000 marines were in position for a final attack. It was a day filled with fierce hand-to-hand combat. The marines continued to blast away at the hidden defenders.

The Third Platoon, Easy Company, Second Battalion, 28th Regiment, 5th Marine Division made its mark on history that day. Commanded by Lieutenant John K. "Ghengis Khan" Wells, this brave group of "just plain ordinary guys" took the lead as the battalion slowly fought its way toward

Suribachi. By day's end they were no longer "ordinary"—
they were heroes.

One man, Private First Class Donald J. Ruhl, earned the
Medal of Honor as he gave his life to save his comrades.
Two men were awarded the Navy Cross; one received the
Silver Star; seven received the Bronze Star; and 17 received
the Purple Heart for wounds received that day. As day
three drew to a close, this battered but most decorated
platoon in marine history was ready for the final assault on
Mount Suribachi.

The Climb to the Top Begins

D-plus three, February 22, 1945, was the fourth day of
the invasion of Iwo Jima. Under rain-filled clouds the 28th
Marines struggled closer to their target. On the west the
Third Platoon had found a path and a small patrol had
climbed partway up the steep, sandy slope.

On Mount Suribachi over half of its defenders were dead
or wounded. This courageous band of Japanese continued
to fire their remaining weapons spasmodically at the attacking marines. The end was in sight.

By the end of day four the 28th Marines welcomed the
darkness. Under cover of night and bad weather there were
few Japanese attacks. By morning the seas were calm and
reinforcements were being landed and casualties evacuated. But the toll in dead and wounded for all marine units
on Iwo Jima had continued to climb. In four days of battle
some 4,500 men had been killed or wounded.

The Final Assault

Early on the morning of day five the 28th Marine Regiment received its final orders. The unit was to climb Mount
Suribachi that day. Battalion Commander Lieutenant Colonel Chandler W. Johnson sent for Lieutenant Harold Schrier,
the new commander of the heroic Third Platoon. He had
replaced Lieutenant "Ghengis Khan" Wells who had been
wounded.

The Stars and Stripes wave over Iwo Jima after U.S. Marines had fought their way inch by inch to the top of Mount Suribachi.

Colonel Johnson handed Lieutenant Schrier a small American flag. His only orders to the Third Platoon were to climb Mount Suribachi, secure the peak and raise the flag. The path to the top was clear and the guns of the fleet held their fire as a small group of 28 weary marines began their slow climb to the top.

Moving cautiously, the platoon received no enemy fire. With guns at the ready, scraping and crawling their way upward, the foremost of the brave young marines soon reached the top. There was no sign of the enemy.

As the rest of the platoon reached the top, one Japanese defender was sighted and quickly shot. Some hand grenades were thrown from nearby caves and a quick firefight developed. The brief Japanese attack was stopped as the defenders retreated into their caves. The marines found a long piece of pipe. They quickly tied the flag to it and the Stars and Stripes was soon rippling in the breeze on the top of Mount Suribachi. It was 10:20 A.M., February 23, 1945. The first piece of a native Japanese island was finally captured and under control of American forces.

Chapter 5

IWO JIMA
SURRENDERS

In spite of the early victory at Mount Suribachi the battle for Iwo Jima was far from over. The Japanese defenders were resisting the marine advances bitterly. They still controlled the northern two-thirds of the island. On February 24 all marine attacks were aimed northward. The main airport was captured and cleared. The first B-29 made an emergency landing on the island on March 4.

Meanwhile, Japanese kamikaze attacks began in great numbers. The word *kamikaze* in Japanese means "divine wind." Japanese aircraft and pilots were assigned to fly suicide missions. The aircraft were loaded with high explosives and the pilots given their instructions to crash their aircraft into U.S. Navy ships. At the height of the attack on Mount Suribachi, a flight of 28 Japanese kamikaze aircraft attacked the U.S. invasion fleet. Five vessels were hit, including two aircraft carriers. The USS *Saratoga* was badly damaged and the USS *Bismarck* was sunk. Some 500 American sailors died.

Iwo Jima Advances Continue

During the last days of February the marines advanced steadily. Sherman tanks were used to support the advancing troops as they crept forward. The reinforced underground installations of the Japanese had resisted the heavy bombardment from the sea and from the air. Japanese troops seemed to spring up out of nowhere to attack the heroic U.S. Marines. Casualties were high on both sides.

Artillery of the U.S. Marines 4th Division shell carefully concealed Japanese positions as the infantry moves inland from the beaches.

By March 1 the U.S. forces had captured about half of the island including a second airport. Over 80,000 marines were now ready to complete the final task of wiping out the remaining Japanese defenders. In the face of suicidal banzai charges the marines advanced.

Although the fighting against hidden Japanese would continue for months, by March 14 the island was declared secure. This announcement seemed premature as there would be 6,000 more marine casualties before the final Japanese defeat two weeks later.

Hidden enemy strongholds with names like Bloody Gorge, The Meat Grinder and Cushman's Pocket still had to be taken and more Japanese wiped out. USAAF P-51s and navy Hellcat fighter aircraft flew close air-support missions, blasting the enemy.

Most of the remaining Japanese were trapped at the extreme north end of the island. Tanks led the way for the U.S. Marine infantry. With rifles, bayonets, grenades, flamethrowers and satchel charge explosives, the infantrymen that followed carried the fight to the enemy to bring the bitter battle to an end.

The losses to the U.S. Marines were terrible. Entire battalions ceased to exist as the number of killed and wounded was so great that the units could not function. Officers and enlisted men alike fell to the fierce resistance of the remaining Japanese defenders.

Twenty-seven marines were awarded the Medal of Honor during the Battle of Iwo Jima. Acts of heroism abounded. Private George Phillips was awarded this highest honor posthumously after he gave his life when, to save his two companions, he fell on a Japanese hand grenade as it exploded. Another Medal of Honor winner was Private Franklin E. Sigler. His citation read, "he led a bold charge, then, disregarding his own wounds, he carried three comrades to safety and returned to fight on until ordered to retire for treatment." The names of all 27 heroes have found a special place in Marine Corps and U.S. military history.

Air Force Begins Operations from Iwo Jima

The main Iwo Jima airport had been repaired quickly. Navy Seabees (Naval Construction Battalions) and Army Engineers put the airstrips in shape for full-scale operations. Some 2,400 damaged B-29s landed there during the months ahead, saving the lives of nearly 25,000 air force crew members. And P-51s stationed there were able to escort and protect the B-29 Superfortresses on their raids on Japanese cities.

The Final Days

On March 26, following five weeks of intensive battle, the Japanese launched one last well-planned assault on the advancing Americans. Attacking silently just before daylight, they overran a large group of sleeping Americans, killing and wounding many. But the Americans soon regrouped and fought back.

U.S. Marines using explosives to blast Japanese from a cleverly concealed blockhouse.

Over 1,000 Japanese participated in this final effort. Most of them were killed. Many followed *Bushido*, the Japanese code of honor, and committed suicide rather than surrender. Of General Kuribayashi's original force of 22,000, fewer than 250 surrendered to be taken prisoner. The general himself committed suicide.

The Americans had lost some 7,000 killed and 19,000 wounded. In addition there were several thousand cases of combat fatigue. It was the most costly battle of the war, as some even said, "the worst since Gettysburg."

Chapter 6

OPERATION ICEBERG — TARGET OKINAWA

The large island of Okinawa, in the Ryukyu chain 350 miles south of Japan proper, was needed to provide the United States forces with a base from which to launch the planned attack against the Japanese islands. The capture of Okinawa would also cut off Japan's supply lines from the south and west. The U.S. Joint Chiefs of Staff had ordered the capture of Okinawa to take place in March of 1945.

As 80,000 marines were engaged in the capture of Iwo Jima, an even larger force was being trained for Operation Iceberg. Veteran army General Simon Bolivar Buckner was in command. The invasion was to start April 1, 1945—April Fools' Day and Easter Sunday. More than 180,000 army and marine troops would participate.

Over 1,500 ships were involved. Admiral Raymond A. Spruance was in overall command of the operation while Vice Admiral Richmond Kelly Turner commanded the amphibious forces that would bring General Buckner's troops to the beaches of Okinawa. The landings were to take place on an eight-mile-long stretch of beaches on southwest Okinawa.

Japanese Well Prepared

The 32nd Japanese Army of more than 100,000 men, commanded by General Mitsuru Ushijima, was stationed on Okinawa. Colonel Hiromichi Yahara was the chief planning

Fire fighting aboard the USS Saratoga *following a successful kamikaze attack on the flattop off the shores of Iwo Jima.*

officer and Lieutenant General Isamo Cho was chief of staff. These highly skilled Japanese commanders were ready to fight off an invasion.

General Ushijima believed that the Americans would land on the southern end of the island. He proceeded to build defensive positions there. Instead of trying to take the offensive as the U.S. forces landed on the beaches, he planned defense in depth. Artillery placed well back from the coast would be able to blast the American forces as they attempted to move inland.

Kamikaze Forces Enlarged

The Japanese fleet had been almost completely destroyed in earlier battles. General Ushijima could expect to receive no help from the Japanese navy. As a result the Japanese high command decided to unleash a huge force of kamikaze aircraft. They gathered some 4,000 aircraft and pilots on the southern Japanese island of Kyushu, 350 miles to the north of Okinawa.

Aware of this plan, U.S. Navy aircraft carriers conducted major air raids on kamikaze bases. Heavy damage was inflicted but 2,000 Japanese planes and pilots were still available. Each kamikaze aircraft would be loaded with up to two tons of explosives and each pilot was prepared to die as he dove his plane into a U.S. ship.

The kamikaze plan for the defense of Okinawa — operation TEN-Go—called for the kamikaze pilots to concentrate on hitting warships first and transports second. There would be ten separate major kamikaze attacks. By eliminating the heavily armed U.S. warships and aircraft carriers, the U.S. transports and landing forces would become easy targets. Some 300 *kaiten* (suicide) boats were also ready to attack the invaders.

The Battle for Okinawa Begins

The Japanese high command rightfully believed that Okinawa would be the next target. On March 22 and again on March 25, U.S. minesweepers and teams of frogmen (underwater demolition experts) went to work near the Kerama Islands just 20 miles west of the Okinawa beaches. They also cleared mines near the landing zone on Okinawa. On March 26 American forces captured the Kerama Islands, destroyed the suicide boats there and set up U.S. supply bases.

Realizing that the attack on Okinawa was about to take place and that Operation TEN-Go was not yet ready, Admiral Matome Ugaki was ordered to unleash a smaller kamikaze attack against the main U.S. Navy defensive fleet, Task Force 58. Although the Japanese lost 160 of the 193 planes used in the attack, some of the attacking armada, which included 69 kamikazes, got through U.S. defenses. Four U.S. carriers were seriously damaged, including the aircraft carrier *Franklin,* which lost 724 crew members that day.

The Japanese put Operation TEN-Go into effect on March 26. Planes took off from Kyushu, from Kadena airport on Okinawa and from Formosa. In the five days before the U.S. invasion, the Japanese kamikaze scored hits on seven U.S. warships including the battleship *Nevada* and Admiral

A huge U.S. task force carves out a beachhead on Okinawa. Landing craft unload men and equipment as battleships, cruisers and destroyers stand off shore to provide protection from enemy attacks.

Spruance's flagship, the cruiser *Indianapolis*. Although there were many casualties and ships were damaged, none were sunk.

Landings on Okinawa Begin

During the same time, U.S. Navy warships carried out a five-day shelling of the landing area on Okinawa. Frogmen continued to clear minefields and underwater obstructions from the beaches chosen for landings. On April 1, 1945, the invasion of Okinawa began.

Little resistance was met as wave after wave of landing craft approached the beaches. Led by amphibious tanks, thousands of soldiers and marines hit the beaches. The landing came off with only slight opposition. Over 50,000 men were landed with their accompanying mountains of supplies.

Other than the confusion of landing so many troops in a short time, the invasion went off without a hitch. Although some Japanese soldiers and civilians were killed, most had retreated inland or hidden in caves.

As night fell on April 1 the U.S. commanders were still

waiting for the Japanese attacks to start. Units linked up and sent out patrols expecting the Japanese to execute banzai attacks. But nothing happened. The U.S casualties at the end of day one were only 28 men killed and some 140 wounded.

General Ushijima and his staff watched from their headquarters at Castle Shuri as the invaders came ashore. They were waiting patiently for the right moment to commence their own offensive.

Advances Continue Unopposed

On April 2 and 3 the U.S. Marine 3rd Amphibious Group under Major General Roy Geiger moved rapidly northward from the beachhead. The U.S. Army XXIV Corps commanded by Major General John R. Hodges moved southward and set up a strong defense line that stretched across the entire island.

Following limited contact with the enemy, both forces continued their advances on April 3. They both reached points they were not to have taken for another seven days. The big question was, "Where is the enemy?" By the close of April 3 U.S. forces controlled a beachhead 15 miles long and a defense line reaching right across the narrow island.

Japanese Begin to Fight At Last

The southern portion of the island was made up of a series of low limestone cliffs filled with hundreds of caves and was ideal for a defensive action. There General Ushijima prepared his defenses in depth across the narrow south-central portion of the island. His first line of defense was a strong outpost line that first stopped the advancing Americans on April 3. Behind this front line was a series of stronger defenses backed up with carefully concealed heavy artillery. Close to 100,000 heavily armed Japanese troops were stationed in this small area waiting for the order to counterattack.

U.S. soldiers blast a hidden Japanese position on a hillside on Okinawa.

Every Japanese unit had been carefully placed. Automatic weapons units were in forward positions to meet the advancing Americans with machine gun and light artillery fire. All roads leading south were thoroughly covered by hidden Japanese pillboxes, trenches, caves and other underground positions.

Iron Resistance Develops

General Hodge ordered his troops to move southward on April 3. It was then that they met their first strong Japanese defenses. Two U.S. Army infantry divisions at full strength took three days to advance less than three miles, receiving strong enemy fire that began to inflict heavy casualties. They had just begun to encounter the strongest Japanese defense lines. As the American troops began their advance toward the Japanese headquarters at Shuri, heavy fighting broke out at last.

More TEN-Go Attacks Unleashed

On April 6 and 7 Admiral Soeumu Toyoda, commander of the Japanese Combined Fleets, ordered a TEN-Go air attack. Kamikaze attacks were carried out against huge U.S. troopships, landing craft and escorting warships.

The flattop USS Randolph *was seriously damaged by a kamikaze attack during the Japanese operation TEN-Go.*

Some 700 Japanese aircraft were sent aloft to attack the U.S. fleet. Of the attacking planes, 355 were kamikazes. Twenty-eight U.S. ships were hit and three of those were sunk. The aircraft carrier *Hancock* and the battleship *Maryland* were among those hit by kamikazes, resulting in heavy casualties.

At the same time the world's largest battleship, the *Yamato*, leading a special attack force, acted as a decoy to draw the U.S. fleet within range of the kamikazes. Before it could even fire its mighty 18-inch guns in combat for the first time the *Yamato* was discovered by aircraft from Task Force 58. Navy Helldiver and Avenger dive-bombers and torpedo planes attacked. The world's mightiest warship was sent to the bottom on its first and only mission. Over 3,000 members of its crew drowned.

As the kamikaze and sea battles drew to a close that day the U.S. fleet was badly shaken by their losses. Little did they know that the attack they had just undergone was only one of ten kamikaze missions of TEN-Go that were to take place.

Chapter 7

OKINAWA'S FINAL DAYS

On April 9 the U.S. forces began their attacks toward the main Shuri defense line. This was the beginning of one of the costliest and most drawn-out battles of the war. For the next four days the 96th Infantry Division attacked again and again. Beaten back and with heavy casualties they made no headway.

To the north, however, General Geiger's marines were met with little opposition. Soon the entire northern two-thirds of Okinawa was in American hands. The marines were ordered south to join in the main battle.

General Cho Calls for a Major Attack

Receiving reports from the Imperial High Command that Operation TEN-Go missions were succeeding, General Cho ordered an immediate attack. For two days Japanese units infiltrated the American lines to assume their attack positions. On the morning of April 13 the Japanese artillery began a heavy barrage. Japanese battalions and smaller units began attacking all along the U.S. lines. Sporadic fighting continued throughout the day with heavy losses to both sides. But the Japanese attack had been poorly planned and coordinated and was soon driven back. The counterattack ended on April 14.

Navy Defense Against Operation TEN-Go

Admiral Mark A. Mitscher knew that the only way to combat the kamikazes besides destroying them on the ground was to intercept them before they reached their targets. To do this he established a ring of 18 destroyers around Okinawa to serve as picket ships. Equipped with radar, they could locate attacking kamikazes as soon as they came into range and direct navy Hellcat and Corsair fighters to intercept them. The picket ship network was responsible for increasing the number of kamikazes shot down.

The Slow Deadly Battle Continues

Meanwhile the U.S. Army and U.S. Marines were suffering mightily. It took eight miserable weeks of fighting for the U.S. forces to capture the Okinawa capital of Naha. This key city was less than 15 miles from the original beachhead. The castle command post of General Ushijima at the town of Shuri was not taken until May 29 when it fell to the U.S. 1st Marine Division. Victory was still almost a month away.

Other battles in the island-hopping campaigns had caused heavy casualties. But none had subjected the combatants to several months of continuous fighting without relief. The U.S. forces suffered over 26,000 noncombat casualties from disease and combat fatigue from April 1 to June 30, 1945. Of these some 14,000 soldiers, both young men fresh from civilian life and combat veterans suffered mental and emotional breakdown.

Opposing Generals Die

As the battle for Okinawa continued on into June both sides suffered tremendous losses. The Japanese, having lost over 50,000 men, withdrew to the southern tip of the island. Battle-weary U.S. troops followed the Japanese retreat carefully, fighting every inch of the way. Finally, on June 18, as victory was almost at hand, the U.S. commander General Buckner was fatally wounded. He was the highest-ranking American general killed in combat in World War II.

On June 20 the fighting stopped. Japanese troops began

A U.S. Marine of the 1st Marine Division draws a bead on a Japanese sniper with his tommy-gun as his companion ducks for cover.

to surrender voluntarily. It was the first time that this happened and it showed that many Japanese were ready to quit. A few days later General Ushijima, knowing that he was finally defeated, committed *hari-kari,* disemboweling himself with his own sword.

One of the major strengths possessed by the Japanese had been their kamikazes. During the period from March 26 until June 22, some 1,500 kamikaze attacks had been made against U.S. ships. Thirty-six ships had been sunk, 26 by kamikaze attacks. Many other ships had been hit and severely damaged, with great loss of life.

The Costliest Operation of the Pacific War

General Ushijima's skill as a general plus the TEN-Go kamikaze operation made the battle for Okinawa the most costly one of the war in the Pacific. The Japanese army fought a carefully planned holding action that stretched the campaign out for almost three months.

Due to the success of the kamikaze attacks 4,900 sailors were killed on the ships that were damaged or sunk. The ground forces on Okinawa received heavy battle casualties also. Total U.S. casualties during the Okinawa campaign, both combat and noncombat, totalled in excess of 60,000 with some 12,000 killed.

The Japanese losses were far greater. Over 100,000 Japanese died. An unknown number of civilians also died during the bitter battle for southern Okinawa.

The losses in U.S. equipment were staggering as well. Almost 500 aircraft were lost in combat and another 250 on the ground. Several hundred tanks were lost during the ground battles and 36 ships were destroyed by kamikaze attacks alone. Some 360 U.S. Navy and Royal Navy ships were damaged. Meanwhile the Japanese had lost all of

Finally realizing that the war is lost, one Japanese soldier, instead of fighting to the death, surrendered.

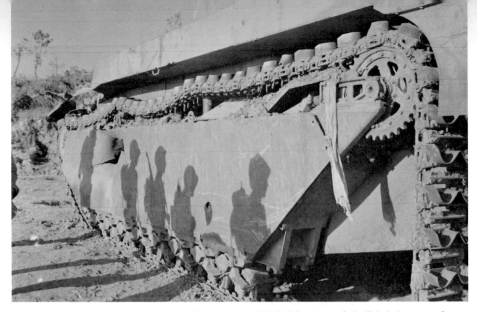

The Okinawa sun casts the shadows of U.S. Marines 6th Division as they move southward on Okinawa to mop up the last resistance.

their ground equipment on Okinawa, some 4,000 aircraft and a battleship.

After General Buckner was killed, General Joseph "Vinegar Joe" Stilwell took over command of the U.S. 10th Army on Okinawa. General Stilwell had served as commander in chief in Burma and China from 1942 to 1944. His first task was to convert Okinawa into a huge supply and staging area from which the attacks on Japan would be launched.

At the same time the Japanese were rebuilding what remained of their army, navy and air force and assembling a vast civilian army to fight the coming invasion of Japan. A battle on the Japanese home islands would be far more costly than on Okinawa and would be disastrous for both sides. U.S. landings on the island of Kyushu were planned for November 1945.

* * * * * * * * *

Yet the invasion of Japan never took place. The end of the war would come in September 1945 following the dropping of the atomic bomb, and World War II itself would join Iwo Jima and Okinawa in history.

Ready for battle, a U.S. Marine awaits the order to attack.

A Closer Look At . . .
MARINES AT WAR

Eyes filled with determination, a U.S. Marine faces the enemy — or death.

His face covered with the grimy sands of Iwo Jima, a wounded U.S. Marine returns to a transport after two days and nights of battle.

This marine, a member of the "Fighting Fourth Marine Division," threatens the enemy even in death.

FAMOUS LEADERS

(Above) Vice President Harry S. Truman (left) and President Franklin D. Roosevelt discuss the war against Japan just before President Roosevelt's death in April 1945.

General Simon Bolivar Buckner (left) discussing plans for invasion of Japan with navy Admiral Richard K. Turner, (center) and marine General Oliver Smith (right).

GLOSSARY

air raid An attack by enemy aircraft.

aircraft carrier A large, flat-topped ship on which aircraft take off and land.

Allies The nations that joined together during World War II to defeat Germany, Japan and Italy: France, Great Britain, China, the United States and the Soviet Union.

anti-aircraft Large cannon or machine guns used to shoot at attacking aircraft.

artillery Large weapons such as cannon, howitzers and missile launchers suitably mounted and fired by a crew.

battleship The largest modern warship.

cruiser A high-speed warship, next in size to a battleship.

destroyer A fast, small warship armed with guns, torpedoes and depth charges.

dive-bomber A plane that aims its bombs by diving.

flamethrower A device used to throw a jet of flaming jellied gasoline at an enemy target.

mine An explosive device placed in a concealed position underground or underwater to destroy enemy personnel or equipment.

napalm A combination of fatty acids that when mixed with gasoline makes a jelly used in flamethrowers and incendiary bombs.

pillbox A concrete emplacement for a military weapon.

radar Radio equipment that detects airplanes and ships and determines their distance, speed and altitude. Short for RAdio Detection And Ranging.

satchel charge An explosive-filled small container used by demolition squads to destroy enemy positions.

strafe To fire machine guns at ground targets from low-flying aircraft.

torpedo A self-propelled underwater missile that explodes on impact with a target.

torpedo plane An aircraft equipped to carry and launch a torpedo while in flight.

INDEX